E X

KINGDOM
PRESENCE
of GOD

EXPERIENCING

the

KINGDOM
PRESENCE
of GOD

*The Character and Essence
of God's Will*

JOHN *and* JANE FICK

KINGDOM PRESENCE PUBLISHING
Blandon, PA

Published by Kingdom Presence Publishing
315 Hope Drive
Blandon, PA 19510

Publisher's Cataloging-in-Publication Data
Fick, John.

Experiencing the Kingdom Presence of God : [the character and essence of God's will] / by John and Jane Fick.
[Blandon, PA : Kingdom Presence Pub., 2005]

p. ; cm.
ISBN 10: 0-9765464-0-X
ISBN 13: 978-0-9765464-0-5

1. Kingdom of God. 2. Jesus Christ—Kingdom. 3. Spiritual life—Christianity. I. Title. II. Fick, Jane.

BT94 .F53 2005
231.72–dc22   2005-925029

Book production and coordination by Jenkins Group, Inc
www.bookpublishing.com

Pen drawings by David Fick
Interior design by Debra M. Beck
Cover design by Kelli Leader

Printed in the United States of America

09 08 07 06 05 • 5 4 3 2 1

CONTENTS

INTRODUCTION

THE DANISH PHILOSOPHER Soren Kierkegaard used to tell a story about a shop in old Copenhagen with a large "Pants Pressed Here" sign in the window. However, if any man in need of such a service would visit the shop with his assorted trousers in a sack, he would soon be seen walking away, disappointed, with the same sack in hand. Why? Because it was only the sign that was for sale, and the shop provided no other types of service but the selling of signs.

Today the church of Jesus Christ is in danger of a similar charge. The sign "Kingdom of God" is displayed in the window, sung through the sanctuary, and sloganed from the pulpit. Our fellow believers and our fellow man yearn for kingdom knowledge and kingdom service. It is the reason that the church exists; yet the kingdom is seldom seen as the primary evidence of Christ's continued presence in the world.

Sadly, kingdom awareness is not a priority with many in the church. "Kingdom" is often an empty term or perhaps a pseudo-prophetic speculative idea. In this age, men have divided, minimalized, and fictionalized the concept of the Kingdom of God. A trivialized message designed for mass consumption

and personal preference has displaced the unity
and integrity of God's kingdom call. This should
not be so. Instead of allowing the context of the
scriptures to connect them to Christ's purposes,
many modern-day believers have chosen to seek just
about everything else but the kingdom. We must
move beyond this tendency of human ambiguity
and press forward into a place of godly precision.

The Kingdom of God is the supreme purpose of
God's creation. It is the majestic and absolute reality
that informs and shapes all things (1 Corinthians
15:24-25, Revelation 11:15, Matthew 6:33). The
purpose of this book is to offer honest evidence
of the essential character and presence of God's
kingdom and your unique place in it. Hopefully,
it has value and meaning for your spiritual life.

KINGDOM AWARENESS

*"For in Him we live and move
and have our being…"*[1]

ACTS 17:28, FIRST SECTION

*"Jesus answered him, "If a man loves me,
he will keep my word, and my Father
will love him, and we will come to him
and make our home with him."*

JOHN 14:23

WE WERE CREATED in the image and likeness of an eternal King. Yet, we live our days immersed in the imaginings of fools. How can this be? How can this be changed?

From the beginning, it has been God's will for all of us that we understand our place in His creation and in His kingdom. It is His desire for every person to experience His redemptive love and creative presence and to receive eternal life. We know this to be true because He extends His Word and Spirit to all humankind with the promise of assured guidance and understanding.

1 All scriptures are RSV unless otherwise noted

His scriptures proclaim an earth and cosmos that are in an essential state of vital obedience and resplendent awe to the creator God:

> *"The earth is the Lord's and the fullness thereof, the world and those who dwell therein..."*
>
> PSALM 24:1

> *"The Lord reigns: let the earth rejoice..."*
>
> PSALM 97:1

> *"The heavens are telling the glory of God; and the firmament proclaims His handiwork."*
>
> PSALM 19:1

Note the wonder and confidence embedded in these Psalms. Yet our perception of creation and God's will and desire for us is often confused and muddled. Why does this happen?

The scriptures describe the creation of God's image-bearers, Adam and Eve, whom God placed in the midst of His garden. They were uniquely loved and qualified to produce an enduring place of fellowship between the living creator and all of His creation. We know that in this endeavor they allowed their minds to become darkened by a pleasing lie and thus they failed as the primary guardians of God's ongoing plan for life on earth.

The awareness that most of us possess concern-

ing the results of this failure is all-pervasive. We
see the results of humankind's fall in everyday life,
in every sphere of human activity. The tensions
that exist between all of humanity and the rest of
creation, between human beings themselves, even
between members of the same family, are real and
dramatic. It is the stuff which tragedy, contradiction,
and despair are most often made of. But there is also
the stuff of hope and heroism mercifully mixed in so
that men might not lose all sense of their first calling
from God.

In this age we have difficulty sorting out the
things of God because we as human beings have
been damaged by sin. This sin of Adam is replicated
in each life as we co-mingle the gifts of God with
an agenda of our own selfish and limited choosing.
Our ideas about God, about right and wrong, often
become confused with motives and desires that
we have already made a priority for ourselves. The
plain truth is that most of us don't want to have to
"choose" anything about God; we want to fabricate.
We want to live as if all that has happened in creation
and in history before us is simply fascinating stage
dressing for our own personal melodrama. We want
to be responsible for nothing except seeing to it that
our many "dreams" come true (Proverbs 14:12).

In such an age of utmost selfishness and spiritual

narcissism we erect a screen of indifference to God's true and proclaimed purposes; we come to relax in the expansive shade of self-image and self-will. And man-made religious doctrines can act as one of the greatest screens of all.

The problem with the doctrines of men, even Bible-inspired doctrines, is that it is possible to condition our thinking with preordained methods of understanding God's word. Nowhere in history is this more sadly shown than it was with the insistence of the religious leaders and scholars of Jesus' own time that Christ be handed over to the Romans and crucified. Their "expertise" in religious matters provided them with an ample education and a comfortable living in a harsh land, but it in no way prepared them to truly understand the nature of the laws, promises, prophecies, and scriptures with which they were entrusted. Like Adam and Eve before them, they allowed their minds to become darkened by the lies they told each other. But our loving Father would not abandon us to such false-hoods; He calls us to a new way of living:

> *"Yet God so loved the world He sent his only son that whoever believes in Him should not perish but have eternal life."*

> JOHN 3:16

Eternal life described in this scripture is not simply the length of life one receives from Christ; it is a quality of life that begins the moment one is born anew as a child of God (John 5:24, John 1:12). Eternal life is kingdom life, a constant participation in the life of God. The song of the Psalmist to *"let the earth rejoice"* now finds agreement and resonance in such a believer's renewed mind and heart.

So why do so many believers resist seeing this kingdom? Why is it that the most compelling preaching on the kingdom often takes place only at gravesides?

God reigns: but men still doubt it. God reigns: sometimes even believers make excuses. God reigns: yet there are those who would like to pass the whole burden of God's revealed will back onto the Jews in some sort of Future Phase II theocratic state. One step forward, two steps back.

Again, why such confusion?

We have allowed the "Kingdom of God" to become a theological debating point. We have stolen from God. We have decided we know what the future should bring, while at the same time enjoying a most pleasant and comfortable present. Instead of dying to ourselves, we have put to death the real-time demands of the Gospel. To see the kingdom, we must believe that it will truly come, just as we are to believe God's will truly will be done on earth as it is in heaven. Such a belief will inspire a new way of living, one that is in communion with one another and a witness to the world—a way of living joined to the thoughts of God.

THE IMMACULATE WILL OF GOD

"For the earth will be filled with the knowledge of the glory of the Lord, as the waters cover the sea."

HABAKKUK 2:14

"This God—His way is perfect; the promise of the Lord proves true; He is a shield for all those who take refuge in Him."

PSALM 18:30

THE PURPOSES OF God are not secret affairs reserved for a special few. They were revealed to us in ages past by the prophets and forerunners of our faith. God's purposes can be verified today by fair-minded people everywhere as they search the scriptures and examine their life experiences.

These purposes, like the eternal God who extends them to us in time, are changeless and perfect.

"So when God desired to show more convincingly to the heirs of the promise, the unchangeable character of his purpose, he interposed with an oath, so that through two unchangeable things, in which it is impossible

> *that God should prove false, we who have*
> *fled for refuge might have strong encouragement*
> *to seize the hope set before us."*
>
> HEBREWS 6:17-18

There is no "Plan B" with God. No alternative promises or strategies with which he cajoles the stiff-necked and self-willed. How would that ever work? And how would such shifting schemes bring glory to the Creator God of the universe?

> *"Many are the plans in the mind*
> *of a man, but it is the purpose of the*
> *Lord that will be established."*
>
> PROVERBS 19:21

> *"Every good endowment and every*
> *perfect gift is from above, coming down*
> *from the Father of lights with whom there*
> *is no variation or shadow due to change."*
>
> JAMES 1:17

God is our rock and His purposes are just as sure and just as solid. His purposes are an extension of His changeless character and immaculate will. We were created as God's image-bearers on this earth and we supplied with God-given talents and intelligence in order to fulfill his purposeful design.

> *"Trust in the Lord forever,*
> *for the Lord God is an everlasting rock."*
>
> ISAIAH 26:4

> *"…When God created man, he made him*
> *in the likeness of God."*
>
> GENESIS 5:1

> *"I cry to God Most High, to God*
> *who fulfills his purpose for me."*
>
> PSALM 57:2

Today, some people talk of God as having two wills, a permissive will and a perfect will. But this is simply bad apologetics and is nonsense. Sometimes when people become confused or frightened by the presence of evil in the world, they willingly give up their confidence in the unity of God's purposes. They simply can't blend their notions concerning the all-knowing, all-good, and all-powerful attributes they assign to God with the manifestation of evil they experience on either a personal or global scale.

Such a bias is totally backwards of the reality it attempts to understand. It is man who has allowed evil into this world and into the collective hearts and minds of a thousand generations. We are the creatures who cultivate, irrigate, and tolerate ill-will towards our fellow man and it is we who have institutionalized indifference to the will of God in this present age. We are responsible for the reservoirs of prejudice and anguish from which all planners of evil draw their perverted inspiration.

Our failure to mature in the knowledge of God's will often produces disaster for ourselves and for those around us. Instead of relying on God, we often settle for the doctrines, precepts, favors, and alliances of man. This is not the way of the Most High.

> "Seek the Lord while He may be found,
>   call upon Him while He is near;
>   let the wicked forsake his way
>   and the unrighteous man his thoughts;
>   let him return to the Lord,
>   that He may have mercy on him,
>   and to our God,
>   for He will abundantly pardon.
>   For my thoughts are not your thoughts,
>   Neither are your ways my ways says the Lord.
>   For as the heavens are higher than the earth
>   So are my ways higher than your ways
>   And my thoughts than your thoughts."
>
> ISAIAH 55:6-9

God's character is not a bundle of human attributes perfected by good intentions. His ways are known to us only by His grace and revelation that He imparts to His church. His will and power cannot be compartmentalized by man to suit our ideas of how He should act.

The purposes of God are "kingdom purposes." This means that He ordains the setting and sense of all human experience. He has told us since ages past that certain realities will impact our lives in ways that are meant to turn our hearts and thoughts towards Him. Only when the events around us and the thoughts within us are put into a kingdom context will we see the manner in which God operates in time. It is in this context that we will experience the peace of God that surpasses all understanding. And this is the glory of God Most High and Holy becoming God most near and knowable.

> *"But seek first his kingdom and his righteousness, and all these thing shall be yours as well."*
>
> MATTHEW 6:33

> *"Our Father who art in heaven,*
> *Hallowed be thy name.*
> *Thy kingdom come,*
> *Thy will be done,*
> *On earth as it is in heaven."*
>
> MATTHEW 6:9-10

What is the nature of this kingdom that the
Lord Jesus instructed us to put first and to seek
with earnest prayer? And what is the dynamic link
between the performance of God's will on earth
and the realization of His kingdom?

These questions are the core issues of the
Christian faith. They point to the very reason the
Lord Jesus left His place in heaven and became flesh
so that He could become the pioneer and perfector
of our faith.

In this age, men have sought to reduce God's
kingdom to either block diagrams and wall charts or
to an excuse for some cosmic "name it and claim it"
magic show. Both of these representations are aber-
rant and filled with error.

Other scholars have reduced God's kingdom to
some form of restored Israelism. And this is little
more than the continuation of the same erroneous
reasoning of the pre-Pentecost first-century disciples,
those who believed that the fullest extent of God's
purposes could be realized only in a theocratic,
legalistic empire. After Pentecost, such speculation
was soon rejected (1 Timothy 1:4, 4:7).

The victory of Christ is irreversible (Hebrews
12:28, 1 John 5:4). The reign of Christ is fixed for
eternity (Revelation 11:15, Colossians 2:15, Psalm
145:13). God will never again return to dwell in a

veiled box with the blood of animal sacrifice
sprinkled about by the hand of man.

When Jesus declared *"It is finished"* (John 19:30),
and the Father bore witness and demonstrated
approval through the tearing of the temple veil
(Matthew 27:51) and the resurrection of the Son
(Romans 6:4), the shadow reality of the law and
temple worship were forever fulfilled in the one
who is the *"light of the world"* (John 8:12).

The fundamental reality of our faith is that
the will of God is understood and fulfilled only
in the Kingdom of God. His kingdom is the supreme
manifestation of His creative and redemptive presence both now and throughout all eternity.

Kingdom understanding distinguishes our faith
from all the religions and philosophies that attempt
to define the inner nature of God from a human
point of view. Kingdom understanding alone is
aligned with the purposes of God and is therefore
able to present the truth in a context that affirms
God's sovereignty and unity.

Let us then boldly proclaim a scope and working definition of the Kingdom of God that cuts through the confusion and timidity of man:

"The Kingdom of God is the Grace and Power to Reveal the Purposes of God and the Presence of Christ to all men."

As we begin anew with this basic definition, let us ask the Holy Spirit to grant us the power to fully comprehend what is the breadth, length, height, and depth of such a kingdom of divine love (Ephesians 3:18).

In Matthew 25, Jesus told the Parable of the Talents. The central point of this parable is that God's servants are expected to increase the character and content of His kingdom in everyday life. We are commanded and empowered by our Holy Lord to make a difference in the world.

His kingdom is always in the midst of us (Luke 11:20, 17:21) and it is what all believers must seek to enter now, while they have breath within them (Psalms 150:6).

It is here today, and it is for all of us who long to draw near to His throne!

The Kingdom of God is not merely an "Epoch," "Era," or "Episode." It is not a nation state, ethnic group, or a matter of flesh and blood.

It is far more than an elaborate system of beliefs and ideals. It is not an "ism" or an "ology" overwhelmed with the fingerprints of men.

This kingdom is rooted in the character and essence of God's will. It is an expression and extension in time of the inter-trinitarian life of God. It is also the human condition redeemed and placed in the Eternal Christ and restored to the eternal now of God's revealed purposes (Habakkuk 2:14). These kingdom purposes define the organic link between the resurrection of His Son and the daily life of every believer (Colossians 3:1-3).

We must come to know this kingdom as the positive self-disclosure of God in the affairs of fallen humanity. We should accept this revelation with the moral determination to love and obey God before all creation. This revelation knowledge connects and aligns us with God's presence and purposes.

And what are these purposes? How are they described in scripture and how are the sons of men going to see them?

The door is through the New Birth.

THE NEW BIRTH
AND THE
KINGDOM OF GOD

"All thy works shall give thanks to thee, O Lord
and all thy saints shall bless thee!
They shall speak of the glory of thy kingdom,
And tell of thy power,
To make known to the sons of men
thy mighty deeds,
And the glorious splendor of thy kingdom.
Thy kingdom is an everlasting kingdom,
And thy dominion endures throughout all
generations."

PSALM 145:10-13

WHEN EXACTLY WAS it that some religious institutions decided that making known to the sons of men the mighty deeds of God and the glorious splendor of His kingdom was synonymous with preaching human ideas about religion? Who exactly decided that a religion about the Bible was a suitable substitute for the clearly stated purposes of God?

It is no wonder that the world is confused with the 'isms" that masquerade as revelation, such as when modern denominations feel free to reinvent the gospel message in order to feel politically correct or when cults trade off the apostolic traditions for self-styled "prophetic" fantasies. It is no wonder that *disunity* has become a modern-day hallmark of religious experience. When men of God stop preaching the glorious splendor of God's kingdom, they have nothing left to preach about except for the fading splendor of human experience and the amusing anecdotes of human frailty. There is little left to teach but the doctrines of men. In contrast, the psalmist in Psalm 145 is clearly exhorting believers throughout all generations to give thanks, praise, and honor to a King who reigns in splendor this very hour and for all eternity. We are encouraged to reach out to all men with the good news of God's mighty deeds, the mightiest being his Son's triumph on the cross and the majesty of His kingdom's presence. This is a presence that is clearly revealed in a compelling manner before the believer has passed on into heaven. Thus, the kingdom is more than going to heaven, more than some future post-messianic activity on earth, and more than a holy slogan or promise:

> "*Truly, truly, I say to you, unless one is born anew, he cannot see the kingdom of God.*"
>
> JOHN 3:3

> *"Truly, truly, I say to you, unless one is born*
> *of water and the Spirit, he cannot enter the*
> *kingdom of God."*
>
> JOHN 3:5

These are the most astounding and revolutionary words spoken in human or celestial history since God said, *"Let there be light."* These words, these invitations, these commands spoken by our Lord and Savior, are not simply a reflection on how mortal men can "get to heaven." These words turn on the here-and-now reign and kingdom of our Eternal God.

The New Birth is the God-ordained portal that allows His children, His elect, to see and enter the Kingdom of God. This Eternal kingdom extends and fulfills the will and creative presence of God among us even now.

"But Christ is the fulfillment of the law for righteousness to every-one who believes. Christ is not a slave who is merely producing more slaves! *Instead, He is producing sons, brothers and fellow-heirs, all of*

who perform the Father's will."

CLEMENT OF ALEXANDRIA, "KNOWING GOD"

Unless one is born again, the world can often take on the appearance of random forces acting upon chance events. Any attempt to impose meaning or value judgments upon such haphazard incidents can appear as an exercise in self-deception. It is a world where one man's good is another man's evil; one man's holy war is a thousand innocents' holocaust. The closer one moves to the heart of man, the closer one seems to move to the center of chaos (Proverbs 28:26) and self-deceit (Jeremiah 17:9). The religions and religious scripts of men offer only a vague promise of relief and they are often linked to an austere system of works and an imposing hierarchy of beliefs.

The New Birth cuts through the doctrines, precepts, and "isms" of men. The New Birth distills the truth of God's word as it unites us in a creative and redemptive way unto God Himself. We are transformed from creatures of God into children of God, and so we become partakers of the very essence of God (2 Peter 1:4, 1 Corinthians 15:49). The meaning and purpose of God's design becomes our soul's calling and sustenance.

How sad it is that our religious instincts, at times far out of step with God's kingdom calling, have reduced the New Birth to a catch phrase hidden in the sinner's prayer. This is snapshot Christianity at its worst—when the new believer comes forward to see and enter the kingdom of His Father, but often walks away with little more than a brochure about a church denomination.

Thus, there has developed in the church a distortion of emphasis. The third verse of John 3 has become the banner of personal conversion as distinct from kingdom entrance. The first aspect stresses the self and the self's inner sense of well-being. The latter more correctly focuses on God's purposes and glory.

Such was also the misconception of Nicodemus, as it is related in the third chapter of the Gospel of John. Nicodemus was the third wealthiest man in Jerusalem. He was a leader and teacher of the Jews. It was the rightful expectation of the Father that men like Nicodemus and men of his circle, by virtue of their education and authority, would become the core of the coming Messiah's proclaimers and disciples. But this was not to be (John 1:11).

We learn from Romans 4:19 an amazing facet of God's plan: *"Israel was raised up from nowhere, from an old man and old woman, Abram and Sara as good as dead…"* It was God's will that the Jews would be a missionary race, the keepers of both the law and the oracles of salvation. From the lens of the law and temple, all men (Isaiah 56:7-8) were to become aware of the essential character of God's plan of salvation. God was to visit His people. That ancient walk in the garden, when God sought refreshment in the fellowship of His children, now long ago interrupted by sin, would be resumed in grace and wonder as the Son would come and walk through the spiritual vineyard of Israel (Matthew 21:37). God was coming to His own.

Yet when Nicodemus came to Jesus by night, he came as one seeking to reconcile the expectation of the status quo with the astounding works and teachings of this upstart messenger from Galilee. He came on the heels of Christ's first cleansing of the Temple.

That night, Nicodemus would get but one full sentence of flattery out of his mouth (John 3:2). Jesus would have none of it. Jesus knew what was in all *men* (John 2:24-25) and Jesus was not into games (Matthew 11:16-17). If Jesus appears to be dealing roughly with Nicodemus, it is only because he sought to wrestle the complacent attitudes and static notions out of one "who is a teacher of Israel" (John 3:10).

The message of the New Birth and new covenant is of supreme importance in the scriptures of Israel, what we today refer to as the Old Testament (Jeremiah 31:31-34, Ezekiel 36:26-27, Isaiah 43:18-21, Psalm 51:10).

Nicodemus and his fellow rulers and teachers should have been ready for this message. They should have been able to grasp its significance and splendor from the spiritual dimension of the law. The Jews had been instructed to meditate upon the law and God promised to reveal his purposes to them as they drew near to him in faith. Some did so (John 6:68), but many did not (John 12:42-43).

Nicodemus is caught in between. He senses something, but he really doesn't understand what this "teacher come from God" is all about. How does this Jesus fit in with all that is happening about him? There were great conflicts among the Jews themselves as evidenced in the relations between the Pharisees, Sadducees, Zealots, and many other Jewish sects. There was the Roman occupation and the Roman puppet officials with their burdensome laws and taxes. And, of course, there was the evil of man, the presence of sin, and the oppression of disease and death. Judaism was fixated on how one stayed ritually clean throughout all this sin, disease, and chaos so that one's status in the congregation would remain intact.

Christ shows no interest in the status of old, religious, powerful men. Christ commands Nicodemus, and through this conversation He commands that all men recognize the necessity of the New Birth.

Note in the language of John 3:3 and John 3:5 how Jesus begins his instructions with the words "Truly, truly" (RSV) or "Amen, amen/verily, verily" (King James Version). This is of extreme importance. He is not merely saying "Most sincerely"! Jesus is deliberately shaping these commands to Nicodemus so that they have the impact of eternity within them. By his two-fold confirmation of the truth contained in these commands, Jesus establishes their universal application and efficacy. These words represent the fulfillment of all that had been promised to the great prophets (Jeremiah 31:31-34, Ezekiel 36:26-27). These words of Christ to Nicodemus are in fact and in this context thus transformed into creedal statements applicable at all times and to all humankind.

The New Birth is not an option. The New Birth is an extension of Christ's incarnational purpose. He enters time so that man might enter eternity as a new creation born not of blood, nor of the will of man, nor of the flesh, but by God. We receive Him because He first received us.

Christ is the kingdom-bearer come to receive the image-bearers of God. God's purpose is fulfilled despite the errors and folly of men. God's will is done on earth as men and women are born anew into His kingdom.

As believers, experiencing the kingdom presence of God begins with the sincere desire to directly and continually participate in the power and grace that transfigures the world.

Such participation is the genuine mark of a believer. Such love propels our uncontrived and pure devotion to the heart of the Father. This participation stretches and unifies the believer's inner life with the ongoing manifestation of the Spirit and Spirit-directed kingdom service.

> *"God's kingdom can be sought only if it is sought first."*
>
> SOREN KIERKEGAARD

> *"Seek the Lord and His strength, Seek His presence continually."*
>
> PSALM 105:4

RECEIVE THE
KING OF TRUTH

*"Jesus said to him, "I am the way,
and the truth and the life;
no one comes to the Father but by me."*

JOHN 14:6

*"And you will know the truth,
and the truth will make you free."*

JOHN 8:32

*"The Lord is just in all his ways, and kind in all
his doings. The Lord is near to all who call upon
him, to all who call upon him in truth."*

PSALM 145:17-18

"Pure truth could burst the world apart."

NIKOLAI BERDYAEV

THE HUMAN MIND was created to recognize
and process truth. The human spirit was designed
to desire and thrive upon truth. God intended life to
be that eloquent and that simple. It was essential for
the fulfillment of His purpose for us upon this earth.
God's plan for us was to live as His children in a state

of perpetual grace and truth.

Even now, thousands of years distant from the beginning of the human race, we can still get a sense of how it was meant to be. Consider how the human lungs, under normal circumstances, thrive effortlessly upon the earth's atmosphere. Yet these same healthy lungs react almost instantly, even violently, to the presence of smoke, chemical fumes, or particulates. The entire body trembles and shakes as the affected person hacks, coughs, and quickly recognizes the danger and leaves the area of contamination.

This was exactly how the human intellect was meant to react to deliberate deceit and falsehood. The mind set upon God's truth simply could not and would not abide in spiritual error.

But this is not how the "normal" human intellect operates today or has in fact operated for thousands of years.

Today we live under the tyranny of human intellect adrift; human reasoning bereft of the Light of God. Human intelligence operating outside the grace and wisdom of God—what a frightening concept, and what a potential weapon of mass suffering!

How often have we seen it happen in history? Even with the best of intentions, men destroy as they attempt to create, murder as they attempt to save, and corrupt as they attempt to make "perfect." In such a perverse order, dominion over others is seen as being synonymous with heavenly favor.

Fallen human intellect is like some pre-programmed machine run amuck in the world. Our brilliant devices often poison the very world we think we are improving. Our scientific break-throughs usually find military and destructive application first. Instead of mankind fulfilling its purpose as God's image-bearer in the world, man falls further to become the idol-maker, the fear-monger, and the worshipper of self.

Instead of being drawn to truth, men are repelled by it, for they understand the implications of any proclaimed standard separate from that which they have concocted for themselves or their little group (John 3:19, Isaiah 30:10-11, Jeremiah 5:31).

The fact that falsehood can be erected with all the trappings of popular culture and the prepack-aged credentials of modern "scholarship" should not further delude us. This is an old ploy, and it was used extensively by the Nazis as well as the Commu-nists who loved to prostitute science in their efforts to discredit the purposes of God. Falsehood cannot frustrate the design of God (Psalm 94:8-11, 1 Corin-thians 1:20-21, Romans 1:18-23, 2 Corinthians 13:8).

The antidote for falsehood is the truth of God. And God, in His wisdom, does not choose to present

truth to man's fallen, prideful intellect as an intri-
cate belief system or an "ism" of austere behaviors.
Because of God's great love for us and because of
our critical condition, God sends truth as a divine
Person, the Person of Jesus, so that no man might
boast that he figured it all out for himself (as if one
could!) and so that all men and women would have
equal access to the grace and revelation of Christ's
redemptive work and the ongoing ministry of the
Holy Spirit.

Such life-giving truth is the outcome of the
Son's triumphant entrance into time and the Father's
sending of the Holy Spirit in order to transcend the
desperately inadequate perspective of man alone.
The Holy Spirit makes our union with the Son
and the Father a true kingdom reality.

The great scholar in the university, the wealthy
business person, the judge, the politician, the factory
worker, and the laborer in the field—all have the
same, unchanging person of Christ standing before
them, offering God's redemptive love, eternal fellowship, and restorative truth.

Just as oxygen sustains each person every
moment of every day, Christ now stands before
each of us offering eternal life and fellowship to
those who will receive Him into themselves. It is as
simple, as fair, and as humble as breathing (Romans

10:9-10, John 6:37). It is the breath of God returning to the "clay" that rebelled at the potter's touch (Genesis 2:7, Isaiah 45:9, Isaiah 64:8). It is truth returning to the mind of man and the public square (Psalm 25:5, Isaiah 59:14-15).

Think of truth as the oxygen of the Kingdom of God. And just as breathing isn't a one-time event in our lives, the receiving of God's truth in the person of Christ must become a continual and essential aspect of our existence. We must be open to receive the truth of Christ into every circumstance and condition of our daily lives. We must trust the Father and allow Him to establish us in truth right where we live.

As the trees planted by God (Psalm 1:3) by their very nature are used by Him to replenish and refresh the oxygen supply of earth, we who are born anew are "planted" by the Father. By remaining faithful to His calling, we are used by Him to purge spiritual error from the atmosphere around us and hopefully refresh those around us with the blessing of truth.

THE SACRED HISTORY OF THE KINGDOM OF GOD

"For thus says the Lord,
who created the heavens
(He is God!)
who formed the earth and made it
(He established it;
He did not create it a chaos,
He formed it to be inhabited!)
"I am the Lord, and there is no other
I did not speak in secret,
in a land of darkness;
I did not say to the offspring of Jacob,
'Seek me in chaos'
I the Lord speak the truth,
I declare what is right."

ISAIAH 45:18-19

"The plots of God are perfect.
The universe is a plot of God."

EDGAR ALLEN POE

GOD CREATED THE universe as a
unified, organized, and purposeful system. Each

kind of being He created was an expression of His nature. God proclaimed this creation and its inhabitants to be *"very good"* (Genesis 1:31).

Mankind enters the picture as God's image bearer on earth. In Eden, God had prepared a garden, a place of purpose, for man in the midst of creation. This garden was the realm of fellowship between God and man, and between man and creation. The garden was something of a home school for man and an arena of blessed labor. This was where man would work tending the garden, and it was the place where man would grow and learn in the presence of God.

Genesis clearly indicates that God and Adam had a dynamic and on-going relationship. Adam was given sufficient knowledge, skill, and information in order to fulfill his "internship" as God's kingdom representative.

No one (except for God and Adam!) really knows how long Adam was in the garden before God discerned the desire of Adam's heart and made for him a being fit to bear the same image of God and help establish the same garden.

God gave Eve to Adam out of Adam's own body. Paul cites this as a prophetic picture of the church being raised up by the Father out of the body of Christ (Genesis 2:24, Ephesians 5:31, 32).

It is important to remember that Adam and

Eve were sinless. They had pristine mental facul-
ties, unclouded by inherent deceit, unencumbered
by confusion or forgetfulness. Their character was
undiminished by sin and their access to God was
assured. Thus they could not simply be "tricked"
into falling away from God's presence. Sin would
first have to enter into their own minds by their own
choice. Then, and only then, would they have made
themselves vulnerable to the lies of the deceiver.

We really don't know when Adam and Eve start-
ed to fall, but it was likely a process, not simply one
specific point in time. The scriptures tell us in James
(James 1:14-15) that each person is tempted when he
or she is lured and enticed by his own desire.

Thus the desire to break away from God, from
His rule and influence, was first incubated in the
heart of Adam and the heart of Eve. In effect, the
desire of Adam and Eve was to expel God, displace
Him, and extinguish His purposes. It was a wicked
notion first nurtured in secret, then cultivated in
whispers. What was not being properly cultivated
and nurtured was the garden itself, and soon an
unwelcome visitor would be able to find his way in.
In my opinion, it is highly unlikely that Eve would
have even considered the option of displacing God
had she not placed within her mind a real impres-
sion that this would please Adam. Adam had failed

to communicate to her any true or lasting love, trust, or allegiance to God. This made Eve vulnerable to the lies of the serpent. Yes, chronologically, Eve fell before Adam, but I have a feeling that Adam all but pushed her.

The picking and eating of the fruit is essentially the diabolical commencement ceremony of man's fall. Man's sin burst forth from beneath the idyllic surface. Man had fully corrupted his heart, his mind, his helpmate, and their future actions. Sin was now visible. The results of sin could now be known and experienced.

God entered the garden that day seeking the fellowship and love of His image bearers, Adam and Eve. He had come in the cool of the day to participate in man's refreshment.

Instead of finding refreshment (a refreshment our Lord still longs to share with us [Psalm 110:7]), the Lord found man and woman in hiding and in denial. He found a fallen humanity resorting to their own works and notions in order to fashion a "covering" suitable for their newly found sense of self-alienation and nakedness. God found Adam and Eve trusting in their apron of leaves and shamelessly seeking to blame someone else for their failure.

The human condition we all know so well had arrived. We may never know what might have happened if Adam and Eve had fallen on their faces and asked for the forgiveness of God. Perhaps God's whole plan of salvation might have been revealed in a single generation.

But such repentance never occurred. Such trust in the Holy One was never exhibited, and God had no choice but to remove Adam and Eve lest *"He [Adam] put forth his hand and take also of the tree of life, and eat and live forever"* (Genesis 3:22). For in that case Adam and Eve would have become eternally evil creatures.

It was an act of divine mercy to remove Adam and Eve from Eden. For although they would now face hardship, pain, and death, it would be over the curse of death itself that God's creative and redemptive plan would construct a bridge into eternal life and restore all mankind's fellowship with Him (1 Corinthians 15:21). The fall of Adam and Eve actually happened. It is a historical and spiritual fact. All human history, human conduct, commerce, and

behavior confirms the continuing rampage of sin
and sorrow across all the epochs and empires
of man. It also has been confirmed throughout
the conscious lifetime of each and every individual
born of woman except one, our Lord, our Savior
Redeemer, Jesus Christ, who was promised to us at
the very moment sin was first found in man (Genesis
3:15). From the very proclamation of this promise
directly from the heart of God, the Son began to
reveal His kingdom-bearing work.

The fall of man and the salvation plan of God
are the foundational truths of human existence.
Without a clear understanding of the consequences
of man's fall, all human history and all personal
introspection is unfathomable, and all human ideas
and "ologies" inconsequential. The reality of God's
kingdom plan of salvation provides the setting and
sense of all human activity. All human pursuits, all
social movements, be they profane or profound, be
they done knowingly or unknowingly, either affirm
the purposes of God or rally against them.

The world's concept of history is flawed and
incoherent. Men have concocted relativistic and
uneven overviews of human events, and history
has been trivialized into sub-plots within sub-plots.

For the lover of truth, only Christ holds human
history together and only the gospel brings light and

meaning into full view. It is the revelation of God's design that brings all other causes and effects to our understanding.

History, thus understood, is sacred because it represents the move of our Savior God in space and time and because it records the corresponding response and changes within the community of humankind. For some it is a response of rebellion and denial; for others, by the grace of God, it is a transfer from a place of darkness into a Kingdom of Light (Colossians 1:13).

There are no disinterested bystanders in or near the kingdom of God. Everyone participates, whether they know it or not.

Thus there are no easy outs or parallel plots. There are no separate agendas or "Left Behinds." At the end of the age there will be one final gathering and final separation (Matthew 25:31-32). Then the Lord will declare to His image bearers, *"Come, O blessed of my Father, inherit the kingdom prepared for you from the foundation of the world"* (Matthew 25:34).

We who are born anew by God's grace are the children of this blessed promise. As the heirs of this inheritance, and by God's grace and through His Spirit, we can walk by faith in this promise every day (Galatians 4:4-7).

THE CELEBRATION OF THE KINGDOM

"All thy works shall give thanks to thee,
O Lord,
and all thy saints shall bless thee!
They shall speak of the Glory of thy kingdom
and tell of thy power,
to make known to the sons of men thy mighty
deeds
and the glorious splendor of thy kingdom.
Thy kingdom is an everlasting kingdom,
and thy dominion endures
throughout all generations.
The Lord is faithful in all his words,
and gracious in all his deeds.
The Lord upholds all who are falling,
and raises up all who are bowed down."

PSALM 145:10-14

THE KINGDOM OF God is to be celebrated: as it is now, was then, and forever shall be. The Father is well-pleased to honor those who have been rescued to a living hope by His Son's great victory.

Bible teachers often discuss that some, if not all of us, who will enter God's presence will be wearing "crowns" (Revelation 2:10). These crowns are being fashioned now as you and I live out our salvation here on earth. These crowns are not for our glory, nor do they exist as some sort of status beacon for the heavenly beings. These crowns serve one purpose: they will be our "noisemakers" in heaven as we cast them with great aplomb and thunderous result at the foot of our Lord's throne (Revelation 4:10).

Our honor is His honor, first and eternally His. And we will become an eternal audience wherein we can empty ourselves before Him in order to refill the essence of our life in His presence. The eternal life He gives us will be lived out in the throne room of heaven, throughout the heavens, within the gates of the New Jerusalem and upon the new earth. We will enter in and out of these realms by the very "door" (John 10:9) who gave us first entrance into the fellowship of the Father, Son, and Holy Spirit (John 14:15-17).

The celebration and awareness of this kingdom life is to begin now!

> "If then you have been raised with
> Christ, seek the things that are above,
> where Christ is seated at the right hand of God.
> Set your minds on things that are above,
> not on things that are on earth. For

*you have died, and your life is hid
with Christ in God."*

COLOSSIANS 3:1-3

*"Therefore, if anyone is in Christ,
he is a new creation, the old has passed away,
behold the new has come!*

2 CORINTHIANS 5:17

*'I will praise the Lord as long as I live; I will sing
praises to my God while I have being."*

PSALM 146:2

This world is far from perfect (Romans 8:21-23), and we, His people, are far from what God wants us to be (Romans 7:15). But this process of His kingdom overcoming this world (1 John 5:4) is the destiny He shares with us now, by faith, and no believer is disqualified from participating in kingdom awareness, celebration, or implementation.

It is Satan who seeks to condemn us, to rob us of our kingdom understanding (Revelation 12:10). His goal is to reduce the body of Christ to a miserable collection of legalists and schizophrenic sadsacks. His aim is to rob our witness of power and authenticity.

For too long, the contending emphasis throughout Christian teaching and preaching has been on

the subject of keeping or losing one's salvation.
Without getting drawn into a fruitless debate over
pretended representations of the thinking of John
Calvin or Jakob Armineius, let us agree that such an
emphasis as the primary measurement regarding the
presence of Christ within us is totally backwards.

What must be emphasized amongst brothers
and sisters is maturity and discipleship. Let there
be a true maturation process that builds confidence,
character, and commitment within the believer—
commitment to the revealed purpose(s) of God.

The primary measurement of an individual's
walk with the Lord must be the presence of *kingdom understanding* and *kingdom effectiveness* within
them, not the mere absence of "sin unto death."

Do we teach people to swim by constantly and
solely instilling in them the fear of drowning?

Do we teach children to trust us as parents by
describing to them what levels of violence we will
employ upon them should they ever disappoint us
in *any* way, either on purpose or by accident?

Then why do we treat God's children as
deserving a discipleship composed of fear and
endless self-doubt? By using such methods, we
have painted countless thousands into a corner
of self-condemnation.

When we allow this to happen to our brothers

and sisters, we are doing Satan's work for him!
He wants to reduce each one of us to one more
broken-down heap on the side of life's road. He
wants all our time and energy tied up by focusing
on our "personal deliverance"—a deliverance that
has already been accomplished two thousand years
ago. If Satan can reduce our kingdom sense into self-
obsessed gibberish and nonsense, then he will have
sent one more child of God spinning off into the
night perhaps looking for anything or anybody
who will speak smooth things into his heart.

The Satanic goal is to get you spinning, reduce
your kingdom witness, and remove your awareness
of God's grace, joy, and victory which remains close
to you always.

Oh, if our sense of God's presence could be as
ever close to us as our sense of sin's empty claims
upon us! What a backwards state of affairs!

Let us replace self-deception with self-denial.
Let us deny our flesh its pity parties, guilt trips, and
adversarial authority. Our flesh is dead in Christ. Let
us determine to cling to God's redemptive presence
even when we miss the mark.

God will not despise our brokenness, our plight
in bondage (Romans 8:1). He is quick to deliver us,
ever ready to forgive and restore us to our first love
in Him.

Let sin break your heart, but not your hold on God's great promises of mercy! Never permit the influence of sin to obscure your sense of kingdom.

If you do miss the mark, be as bold in seeking His forgiveness as you were in seeking your own way in the first place!

Know the difference between "wickedness" (which is the continued planning of sin and sowing of discord in this life) and the misstep or sudden fall that is all too common for we who are still in the world.

As believers, we are instructed to seek wisdom rather than self-condemnation.

Some would say, "But God views all sins the same."

Thank heaven this isn't true!

Thank heaven He viewed Peter's repeated denials differently from Judas' kiss!

Thank heaven He viewed Paul's acts of persecution differently from those of Herod!

It is Satan who views all human sin the same. As he accuses us and judges us unworthy, he seeks to frustrate our hearts, confuse our thinking, and further pollute our lives with self-pity and doubt.

Let us praise God because we have a Redeemer who extends His grace and righteousness through us even now—and so we can celebrate!

To celebrate is to honor the kingdom by consecrating ourselves to the purposes and promises of God. Such is the way of life that has already been pioneered and perfected for us by our Savior Redeemer, Jesus Christ.

We honor Christ by receiving Him, acknowledging Him before God and man, and by believing and clinging to the character of His finished work on the cross.

True faith, true kingdom celebration in Christ, consists of the constantly renewed realization that it is possible and efficacious to accept the grace of God through Christ. For us, it is the steadfast belief and precious understanding that God is faithful to all who call upon His name in truth.

God will grant you countless opportunities in this life to dare to express just such a faith. They will appear every day, every hour. **Honor your King.**

> *"Therefore let us be grateful for receiving*
> *a kingdom that cannot be shaken,*
> *and thus offer to God acceptable worship,*
> *with reverence and awe..."*
>
> HEBREWS 12:28

KINGDOM PRESENCE

*"It is the glory of God to conceal things
It is the glory of kings to search things out."*

PROVERBS 25:2

*"Seek the Lord and His strength
Seek His presence continually!"*

PSALM 105:4

*"It is a betrayal not to recognize that all history
is moving towards the Kingdom of God."*

JACQUE MARITAN

KINGDOM WAS ALWAYS on the heart of our Lord. Kingdom truth flowed from His lips; Kingdom power and authority resounded in His actions.

The preaching of Jesus proclaimed kingdom (Mark 1:14-15). The parables of Jesus planted kingdom (Matthew 13:10-12). His miracles pointed to the presence of God amongst His people.

Jesus is the Word made flesh (John 1:14). He is the sustainer of the universe and all humankind by His word (Hebrews 1:3, Colossians 1:17).

In this age, it often seems that men seek "truth" in every place but where it is most abundant—in the person of Christ. We seek the "true interpretation" of scripture in every place but where it actually resides: in the person and words of Jesus.

Jesus is the true interpretation of the Bible. His life, His stated purposes, His teaching, and His example fulfill both Testaments and fulfill the eternal unfolding of God's purposes (Ephesians 1:9-10).

From the foundation of the world, there has been One who uphold us, One who knows our name (John 10:14, 27, Ephesians 1:4). Jesus Christ is the kingdom presence (Colossians 1:19). Jesus is the kingdom-bearer who extends the knowledge of God, the very "face of God's glory" (2 Corinthians 4:6) to all who seek God in sincerity and truth.

Sometimes churchgoers seem to think that by quoting some ancient Hebrew title of God (such as El Shaddai or Jehovah Jirah) they are in fact closer to the real nature of God. Presumably, this sounds profound and scholarly to our ears. It can certainly seem interesting. But the plain, simple truth is that there is no higher name, no clearer representation of God's character and purpose, than the name **"The Lord Jesus Christ"** (Ephesians 1:21, Philippians 2:9).

This is the name that is higher than any name in heaven, on earth, and under the earth. This is the eternal name, the eternal honor, and the eternal chorus that will shower all heaven, and the Trinity itself, in glory and splendor.

No secret name of God awaits you in heaven. There is no unknown title that will connect all the dots. The Lord Jesus Christ is the very fullness of deity (Colossians 2:9) now recognized and glorified. The Father, Son, and Holy Spirit are one in purpose, authority, nature, and substance! God is one. The name above all names is one. The Trinity can never be diminished by the completed work of Christ, for it was the completed work of Christ that provided God's people with the full revelation of the Trinity in the first place.

Jesus Christ, true man and true God (Isaiah 9:6). Alpha and Omega, King of Kings (Revelation 22:13). Jesus is the way—the kingdom way. Jesus is the truth—the kingdom truth. Jesus is the life—the kingdom life that unites all creation in redemptive awe before the Father. We are united in this presence before the Father the instant we first believe and respond in love toward Him (John 14:23).

One must never separate who Jesus is from what Jesus does. He is still the kingdom proclaimer. In this age, we are His hands, voice, feet, and eyes. We are the continuum of His incarnational work. We are His body. Consider carefully this parable of our Lord:

> *"The Kingdom of Heaven is like treasure hidden [past action] in a field, which a man found and covered up [past action]: then in his joy he goes and sells all that he has and buys that field [present action!]."*

MATTHEW 13:44

[WATCHMAN NEE, THE KING AND THE KINGDOM OF HEAVEN]

This parable offers a profound picture of the work of our Lord himself. The "man" in the parable is our Lord; the "field" is the world at the time of our Lord's ministry, and the treasure is the souls who would respond to the Father's calling (John 6:37), those who would receive Him and join themselves to the "True Vine" (John 15:1). These are the kingdom's treasure.

(Some Bible teachers like to read this parable backwards by seeing you and I as "the man." This is an unwarranted personalization of the text. How could that work? What are you and I "covering up" before we buy the field from the unsuspecting owner? What could you or I possibly sell in order to buy access to a heavenly kingdom?)

Salvation is not our work or a matter of our sacrifice, but Christ's. We are the ones who have been "bought with a price" (1 Corinthians 6:20).

The central theme of this parable is that the nations and religions that were using the field, the tenant farmers, so to speak (the Jews, Greeks, Romans, etc.), did not have knowledge of the treasure beneath the surface of their world interest. To them, religion was an orchestrated game, and individual men and women were a source of disposable labor and amusement. They failed to recognize the hand of God in the creation around them (Romans 1:20) and the image of God in every human face before them. Likewise, Satan saw nothing of lasting value in the character of man (Job 2:4).

Neither the nations or religions using the field (as bad tenants), or Satan prowling through the field, were the actual rightful owners of the field. That is the right of God alone.

God sent the Son into the world to seek those who were lost, those in need of a "physician." And it was in them that the Son, the true kingdom-bearer, found the treasure fit for His kingdom (Proverbs 25:11). Like an apple of gold in a setting of silver, the redeemed image- bearer of God would be restored to the kingdom presence of God (Ephesians 3:11-12) by the work of the Son alone.

When Jesus found the first of His treasure, His disciples, He hid them in the palm of His hand (John 10:28). Satan demanded to sift them as wheat, starting with Peter, but he could not get at them because the Son stood in their place. Jesus bore the weakness of His disciples throughout His earthly ministry (John 17:12). He kept them, He loved them, and He called them friends even on the eve of their scattering and fearful abandonment of Him.

He covered them up for a season in His incarna-tional shadow in order to cover them eternally in His blood. The field is purchased from our Creator God. And so, with all that He had, Jesus redeems the trea-sure, that treasure being our souls joined with the Father's kingdom purposes. We are now His because He made us, He redeemed us, and He continues to sustain us.

> *"It is the glory of God to conceal things and the*
> *glory of kings to search things out."*
>
> PROVERBS 25:2

Such is the timeless glory of God! His purpose,
His plan, a "mystery" now revealed for all time:

> *"For he has made known to us in all wisdom*
> *and insight the mystery of his will, according*
> *to his purpose which he set forth in Christ as a*
> *plan for the fullness of time to unite all things*
> *in Him, things in heaven and things on earth."*
>
> EPHESIANS 1:9-10

> *"To me, though I am the very least of all saints,*
> *this grace was given to preach to the Gentiles*
> *the unsearchable riches of Christ, and to make*
> *all men see what is the plan of the mystery*
> *hidden for ages in God who created all things;*
> *that through the church the manifold wisdom*
> *of God might now be made known to the prin-*
> *cipalities and powers in the heavenly places,*
> *this was according to the eternal purpose*
> *which he has realized in Christ Jesus our Lord,*
> *in whom we have boldness and confidence of*
> *access through our faith in him."*
>
> EPHESIANS 3:8-12

It is to the Father's glory that He was faithful and just and maintained His covenant throughout the ages. Man sinned, the Patriarchs stumbled, and Israel rebelled, but God was always faithful and did not remove the "treasure" of His kingdom plan, nor the love for His people from the earth. It was hidden from the proud, powerful, and self-satisfied. But it was revealed by the Son, our Savior and Lord, our faithful friend (Proverbs 18:24, John 15:14-15).

The Son, our King of Kings, even now through the Holy Spirit continues to "search out" the treasure hidden in each generation, each human epoch, and reveal to them the eternal will of His Father. It is a search that requires us to go forth to all nations in His name (Matthew 28:18-20).

(Note: There is no small amount of confusion concerning our Lord's statement before Pilate that His kingdom *"was not of this world."* In the context of this pivotal conversation recorded in John 18, note that our Lord never denies His kingship—what our Lord defines once and for all time is the source of His kingdom authority. That is from above. Jesus is speaking of the glory that was His before He came into this world [John 17:5]. No nation, no group of men, had the right to assign "kingship" to the Son. He is the Eternal Son of the Eternal Father. All that is in the Father is in the Son [John 1:18, John 10:10, John 10:37-38.])

In His conversation with Pilate, Jesus is speaking of the source of His kingdom authority, not the scene of His kingdom activity. Throughout the Gospel, Jesus is clear that His presence, His life, and His actions represent the Kingdom of God in operation amongst men (John 5:20-24, Luke 11:20). The Kingdom of God is of heavenly origin, but it is also extended to earthly operation (John 5:17, John 14:12).

If anyone doubts the eternal reign of God, let them meditate upon the songs of Israel. In the book of Psalms, there is a series or category of Psalms known as the "Enthronement Psalms." These are the scriptural proclamations of God's kingdom presence on earth, in the midst of Israel, but for the redemptive and restorative benefit of all mankind (Isaiah 56:7, Psalm 119:64).

Note Psalms 46, 47, 92, 93, 97, 98, 99, 100, and 104. Some of the most powerful statements concerning the eternal character and authority of God are revealed in these scriptural hymns:

> *"Be still and know that I am God*
> *I am exalted among the nations,*
> *I am exalted in all the earth!"*

> PSALM 46:10

"For God is the king of all the earth..."

PSALM 47:7

"The Lord reigns; let the earth rejoice."

PSALM 97:1

*"Make joyful noise to the Lord, all the earth;
Break forth into joyous song and sing praises!"*

PSALM 98:4

*"May the glory of the Lord endure forever,
May the Lord rejoice in His works."*

PSALM 104:31

Read these hymns and learn of your Great Eternal King! Marvel at the power and grace of these scriptures. These Psalms, written many hundreds of years before the birth and ministry of our Lord Jesus, are already celebrating the truth and certainty of God's reign. They celebrate a sovereign presence that the worshippers acknowledged as the here and now reality for them as well as for all peoples and all nations throughout the earth!

The universalism and majesty of these Psalms is stunning. They are without parallel or precedent amongst the ancient religions of that time. God's children are proclaiming a loving, eternal creator God for all humankind. He is a God who desires

to reign in the midst of all people, not just before
the ancient Hebrews who were attending a specific
religious event.

How could such sentiments flow from this tribal
nation operating in a small corner of the world?
The reason is simple: God was in their midst. His
revealed purposes were codified in their laws and
prophets. His Spirit had supplied them with the
scriptures, the history, and the substance of God's
plan of salvation and the very wisdom of God
Himself (Psalm 119:18, Luke 24:27).

The Jews had not been "chosen" as one nation
above all others. Rather God had chosen an old
man and an old woman "as good as dead" (Hebrews
11:12), meaning that they were beyond childbearing
years. He honored their faith in Him and blessed
their descendants in a special way, in a way that was
meant to bless all humankind. Through them He
would make a direct entrance into human history
as the incarnate Savior. He would "set up" salvation
in a way that resounded with authentic credentials
and proofs of identity. (The true purpose of tribal
genealogy, prophecy, and the symbolism embedded
in the law.)

The descendants of Abraham and Sarah were
to hold the oracles of salvation (Romans 3:2) for
all humankind. These scriptures are the very

"credentials" of the Savior, the holy prophecies that were a wonder to the wise throughout all the earth (1 Peter 1:10-12, Matthew 2:2-6).

The Jews were meant to be a missionary race, a race of Jonahs and Nahums who would speak of God's purposes to all the cities and nations. The temple itself was to be known as a house of prayer for all peoples (Isaiah 56:7). Note the very anger of Jesus when He encountered the flea market set up in the temple court of the Gentiles (John 2:14)!

In some instances, the Jews upheld this calling (1 Kings 8:4-43). In other instances they followed it begrudgingly (note the ministry of Jonah). Yet even though the rulers of Judaism turned their back on the commission (Isaiah 59:1-16), God still shaped their national destiny in a way so that His kingdom would be expanded and glorified. Even after the dispersion of the Jews, God would use the scattered synagogues throughout the Mediterranean world as the established beachheads that the Apostle Paul would utilize to present the Gospel message to all humankind in a compelling and valid manner.

And so with the transfer of God's covenant "stewardship" from theocratic Israel to the body of Christ itself (the church), the kingdom presence of God can now be more effectively communicated and represented to all men (1 Corinthians 2:1-5, 2 Corinthians 4:2, John 14:12, 17).

We are responsible for this kingdom presence. It starts in our very personhood, flows through our fellowship life (Romans 12:9-18), and is required by our Lord to empty into the very sea of all humanity. Our Lord identified the needs and conditions of all humankind (sickness, poverty, broken-heartedness, powerlessness) with Himself, so that by emptying ourselves into this body of humanity, we are in a very real sense emptying ourselves into the Lord (Galatians 6:2, Matthew 25:44-45).

Kingdom presence is the character and grace of Jesus revealed in us and through us both as individual believers and as a community of believers as we minister throughout the earth. It is the presence of the Person who upholds all things to the glory of the Father (Colossian 1:17-20).

> *"My presence will go with you,*
> *and I will give you rest."*
>
> EXODUS 33:14

> *"...and lo, I am with you always,*
> *to the close of the age."*
>
> MATTHEW 28:20

THE KINGDOM
OF GOD
VS.
THE KINGDOM
OF THE ABSURD

"…In the world you have tribulations; but be of good cheer, I have overcome the world."

JOHN 16:33

"Christianity is not a matter of persuasive words. It is a matter of true greatness as long as it is hated by the world."

IGNATIUS, LETTER TO THE ROMANS AROUND 110 A.D.

WHAT THE WORLD cannot control or corrupt it seeks to destroy. What the world cannot destroy it seeks to make ridiculous.

This doesn't simply mean that some people will make fun of God's people and His Word. It means that there will be powerful men and women who will conspire in all their societal circles (law, science, entertainment, business, etc.) to make God's sovereignty appear preposterous and bizarre. Believers will be portrayed as poorly educated buffoons, and the church will be stereotyped as hypocritical, morally corrupt, sexually repressed, and hateful. All the ills of countless native cultures will be maliciously back-referenced to the dates when Christian missionaries first showed up, presumably carrying their black, oversized Bibles.

The horrors of child sacrifice, child prostitution, widow burning, exposure of female infants, slavery, fetishism, and dozens of other diabolic practices such native cultures were hopelessly locked into will be glossed over in the attempt to portray all of them as violated Edens. Such is the blatant tomfoolery and psycho-babble of Satan's "cultural war" (now being waged in absentia) as it occurs daily in classrooms, newspapers, and on a cable network near you.

The primary thing believers need to understand is that when Satan or any of his imps are referred to as "gods of this world," it is a rebuke and a mock. It is not true that Satan has any legitimate claim on this planet, the material universe as a whole, or upon the living beings therein. It is also not true that Satan rules in hell, presumably from some oak-paneled, air-conditioned front office. And finally, it is not true that he seeks the worship of men and is willing to buy a single human soul for so much as the price of a retread snow tire.

Satan hates the human race. We are vile and

loathsome in his sight. In his estimation, we are
metaphysical cockroaches that scurry under his feet,
too stupid to avoid the poisons laid before us and
hopelessly averse to dwell in the light.

Satan corrupted his splendor as an image-bearer
of God (Ezekiel 28:17), and now the thought that
this title and birthright has been invested in the
clay of this earth is more than he and his demon
fellow travelers can bear. He loathes us. His maniacal
"plan," his only deluded hope (when, in fact, he is
beyond all hope), is to turn humankind's assorted
cultures, sciences, and religions into such a stench,
such a continuous holocaust in the eyes and nos-
trils of God, that God in an enraged moment will
condemn all life on earth to the abyss. It is Satan's
perverse expectation that a God encumbered by
the burden of making Himself "vulnerable in
time" by committing Himself to the incarnation
of His Son will then be forced to change due to an
expected great outburst of divine anger when men
continually reject His Son's sacrifice. And the result
of this "change" in the inner character of God will
then force a diminishing of God's hold on heaven
and earth. This is Satan's false view of God's
character and power.

At a minimum, Satan wars on to force an
unjustified general amnesty for all sinful beings.

As a wild card, he still considers God vulnerable as long as God extends himself in time and is willing to have the sins of men cast at the foot of His Son. By waging an ongoing war against the church and the nations, Satan pushes forward a continued agenda to raise up Hitlers, Stalins, Saddams, and countless other oppressors of God's people. The horror experienced by the innocents who suffer in this age is also truly endured by a loving, eternal God who upholds all things (Romans 2:4, 1 Corinthians 13:7).

Satan's wicked scheme is that the longer God bows His nature in time, the less able He will be to long endure and sustain the endless flow of grace and mercy required to hold the very fabric of this universe together (Hebrews 1:3).

Satan's rage is real. His desperate schemes are tinged with perverse genius. He has expert knowledge of men and a corrupt but partially accurate knowledge of God's purposes. He was the brightest of God's works, and now his sights are set upon us (1 Peter 5:8). In his thinking he has no chance to escape an all but certain destiny at the bottom of the lake of fire except that the continued outrages of men, especially "believers" on both a personal and global scale, can force the corruption of God's nature during this age of God's transcendent love and grace.

Jesus cried out *"It is finished"* on the cross and

made a public example of the powerlessness of the forces of darkness. Jesus has promised to be with us until the end of the age (Matthew 28:20). Our Lord refrained from calling upon the twelve legions of angels set to "rescue" Him from His hour of trial.

Satan clings to the vain hope that "time" is the single flaw in God's creative and redemptive plan. Satan is a predator striving to exploit any perceived opportunity to diminish God's influence and corrupt God's purposes.

Never has there been such a wicked agenda. It is an agenda fueled by the entire history of evil on this planet. It is comprised of every murder, sin, atrocity, slander, and curse that has flowed from either the hand or mouth of men. Satan may be "bound" (Matthew 12:29) by the kingdom presence of the Holy Spirit in this age, but his agenda (the forces of the gates of hell) is not so bound and is being fueled and refueled almost without ceasing by every wicked act or thought that passes freely from the will of man—believer and unbeliever alike.

No, Satan is not the legitimate God of the planet (Psalm 27:1, Psalm 97:1). In fact, he recoils at the thought of being "honored" with such a prospect. He sees our planet as a dung hill long needing destruction. His perverse sights are set upon something far more significant—Satan wants for himself the same lie he repeated to the itching ears of Adam and Eve: *"Ye shall be as God."*

The failure of modern believers to understand the schemes of the evil one is directly linked to the believer's inability to develop kingdom reasoning and faithfully extend the inherent power and promise contained in the New Birth (John 1:12, 2 Corinthians 5:17, Romans 12:2).

God's kingdom is the bulwark that reduces the feigned and pretended claims of the absurd one. The kingdom message changes the perspective and loyalties of believers and of those under the influence of believers.

Our enemy wages a spiritual battle not merely to get random individuals to commit specific sins and then retreat into the fogbank of guilt. This is also a battle to make the church itself irrelevant, self-absorbed, and bound to ineffective methods and formulas. With the church thus effectively "checked," Satan is free to continue his war on children, babies, the poor, those in prison, the lonely and human DNA itself. In fact, the corruption of the human DNA, the DNA of God's image bearer, has long been a goal of the evil one going all the way back to the crisis experienced in the days of Noah (Genesis 6:1-7).

The absurd one is working overtime in order to

convince large numbers of believers that the condition of this world is not truly their concern once they "get saved." They are being presented with an alternative reality; they will be jettisoned off the planet's surface just in time before Satan is allowed to unleash some type of end-time offensive against…whom? The remaining unbelievers?

My fellow believers, you are here as the incarnational representatives of Christ's character and presence, and you will leave only at that time deemed appropriate by the sovereign will of God.

Christians are responsible for the destiny of the world (Matthew 5:13-14, Proverbs 24:11, II Corinthians 10:5). It is time we wake up to this fact and begin acting accordingly. We must tend the vineyard of our Master prior to His return (Matthew 21:40). He expects an increase of the talents bestowed upon us and entrusted to us as His kingdom representatives (Matthew 25:14-30). The saving of our comfortable skins is not the harvest He desires, nor will He be in any way satisfied with such a meager return (Matthew 25:26-27). The call is for us to proclaim and persevere, not evacuate in mid-harvest.

Faithfulness is the call of Jesus, and no escape clause is embedded in the small print of His kingdom commission (Matthew 25:26-27).

The Kingdom of the Absurd is a realm of fear and hate that has ravaged our planet since the fall. Resist this realm in the power of the One who has overcome all the evil in this world (1 John 5:4-5).

"Resist and rebuke the enemy and <u>he</u> will <u>flee</u> from you." (James 4:7). Get it right the first time and move on to faithful service from there.

The Kingdom of God has *blessed* every corner of the globe that has received it.

The Kingdom of God is the supreme expression of God's love. It is founded upon the life and sacrifice of our Lord Jesus Christ.

Our responsibility towards all mankind coexists with the ministry of Jesus. As His bride, how could it be anything less?

Some Christians would like to write off the remaining percentage of mankind and move on to glory from there. This is not the example of Jesus, and it is not an example of the love that bears all things, believes all things, hopes all things, [and] *endures* all things (1 Corinthians 13:7).

The finished work and the person of Jesus stand undivided and unrivaled throughout all eternity. Our Savior King unites all things in Himself: deity and incarnation, intercession and authority, mediation and rule. The person and work of Jesus must never be represented as scattered throughout diminishing human timetables or as limited by arbitrary human categorical reasoning. We make Jesus less than He is when we try to put Him in a box or customize Him according to our own standards. This happens when we embroider artificial storylines and theories onto the fabric of God's plan.

Before a holy God, let us seek to develop our understanding by meditating on the majesty of Christ's victory (Psalm 145:5). Consider this: While Christ was on the cross, prior to His death, prior to resurrection, prior to His ascension, Jesus bestowed eternal life upon a repentant sinner (Luke 23:43). Who but a King could speak with such authority! Who but a Savior could assure such a place in eternity! Who but a great Savior King could proclaim and set up such a salvation before the foundation of the world (Ephesians 1:4, Revelation 13:8)! Jesus *is* the King of Glory (Psalm 24:8), and He is the King of Kings (Revelation 17:14).

The power of darkness, confusion, and absurdity is crushed beneath the feet of the humble when the humble call upon their Savior King.

KINGDOM REASONING

*"Leave simpleness and live,
and walk in the way of insight."*

PROVERBS 9:6

*"We go towards something that is not yet, and
we come from something that is no more."*

PAUL TILLICH, THE ETERNAL NOW

HUMAN INTELLIGENCE IS shaped by truth, discourse, and compelling comparisons. Humans respond emotionally and intellectually to experience, either their own or those of whom they respect. Scripture is a repository of human experience that can be examined in the light of God's revealed purposes. Scripture provides ample comparisons of the way men and women have responded to the reign of God.

The story of the children of Israel miraculously delivered from the bondage of Egypt and led by Moses toward their Promised Land is a story of divine transformation. It is a series of scenarios where the modes of "thinking" developed in the minds of people while in bondage are constantly

being challenged by the sheer improbability of
God's presence and purpose. The Lord is calling
them to become an entirely new kind of people with
a radically different perspective towards His power
and presence among them.

Time and again, the Lord and His servants must
stand before outbreaks of disbelief and spiritual
rebellion.

It would take the passing of an entire adult generation of the "redeemed" children of Israel before
their corrupt reasoning could be purged from the
community of believers. At least by then, they were
purged to the extent that God would permit Joshua
to lead a new generation over the Jordan.

Let us examine the parallel reality and difference between the kingdom reasoning we are called to
exhibit by our Savior God (Psalm 106:6-45) and the
wilderness thinking that has beset every generation
unwilling to learn and rely upon the ways of the Lord.

NOTE THE FOLLOWING CONTRAST:

Kingdom Reasoning	Wilderness Thinking
■ Seeks God's Purposes (Ps 119:15)	● Challenges authority (Titus 3:9-11)
■ Examines "truth" in the light of the person and completed work	● Clings to the bias and opinions of men, especially "special

of Christ; clings to the Holy Spirit (John 8:12, 14:7, Ephesians 1:13-14)

men" (Jude 1:19)

- Despises the former life (Phil 3:8)

- Prone to mingle their prejudices and opinions with the revelation of God (Psalm 106:35-36)

- Examines only the inner life of the believer (1 Cor 2:11-16)

- Seeks to reintroduce the images and elements of their former life at the first opportunity (Isaiah 1:15, 9:10, 30:1-2, Exodus 32:1, James 4:4)

- Rests in the presence of God (Matthew 11:28-30)

- Constantly compares itself and its situation with others (Proverbs 11:12, 2 Corinthians 10:12)

- Sees eternity in the balance of all human activity (Galatians 6:8)

- Seeks to force God's hand; is oversensitive and accusatory (Isaiah 29:20-21)

- Empties the self for the Glory of God and extends the love of God to all humankind (Philippians 2:3, Proverbs 11:25, Matthew 25:40)

- Thinks small; seeks the minimum (Proverbs 26:15, Ecclesiastes 11:4)

- Sets its thinking on things above (Ps 119:27, Rom 12:12, Col 3:1-2)

- Self-absorbed and legalistic (Proverbs 18:2, Titus 1:15-16)

- Seeks union with God rooted in a contemplative life, service to others, and in the breaking of bread (Isaiah 26:3, Matt 25:40, 1 Cor 11:23-26)

- Combative and restless; annoyed by displays of worship and "brokenness" in others (Mark 14:4, Philippians 2:3)

Today, throughout the community of believers, throughout God's kingdom, a similar false system of "wilderness thinking" is evident. At times such thinking is even encouraged by those eager to exploit the superficiality of men (2 Timothy 4:3).

The above table is not meant to imply that we, as believers, are in fact in a spiritual wilderness. Though at times, individually or collectively, we may pass through a hard season (Ecc. 3:1-9), it is not fitting for us as Christians to see ourselves, as

a whole, constantly in such an abandoned state
(John 7:38, John 10:10).

This age is not "Egypt" or "Canaan" or
"Babylon." We must not waste our time and mental
energies in the speculative controversies generated
by one thousand metaphors of spiritual experience.

This age is the age of "Jesus Christ is Lord"—
receive Him and allow Him to lead you.

The age to come is also the age of "Jesus Christ
is Lord"—we are His now and forever (Ephesians
1:20-21).

Today we are in the vineyard of God, attached
to the True Vine (John 15:1) and tended to by the
Father.

The attached branch is not surprised by the hand
of the Father as He prunes and shapes each one of
us. Beyond the pristine austerity of such pruning lies
the glory of the Son's presence longing to be revealed
in our lives. This is not the desperate application
of wilderness life, but it is the creative application
of those called to crucify the flesh (Galatians 5:24,
Psalm 119:71) and come follow Jesus.

We are of the vineyard of God, tied to the true
vine—our Lord Jesus, who is seated at the right hand
of God. Our spiritual life is nurtured even now from
heaven above.

Hence, we grow in Him as the vital link between

us is maintained by the Father's promise and the ministry of the Holy Spirit.

Such a life no longer sees spiritual things from a human point of view (2 Corinthians 5:16) but sees the hand of God as it moves through all the moments of our life in this world.

Such perception is the foundation of kingdom reasoning.

With kingdom reasoning, all things, including things revealed in scripture and things that happen in our lifetime, take on the dimension of Christ's example and redemptive presence.

Even when we must struggle to find meaning or make sense of a situation or moment, we do not despair because the face of Christ is with us (2 Corinthians 4:6) and His face is the face of God. His revealed presence is greater than any circumstance, and His love sustains the branch through its pruning and affliction (Psalm 119:75, John 15:9).

Kingdom reasoning does not demand to know all things now, for our ability to fully grasp such knowledge remains imperfect. Kingdom reasoning does share in great spiritual truths (1 Corinthians 2:10-13), and greater still, kingdom reasoning is entrusted with the context of God's will—a context that is eternal and is an extension of God's grace and truth.

The context of kingdom is one of the greatest restorative gifts given to the mind of the believer. Without kingdom context, our spiritual thoughts and words are like Christmas ornaments attempting to float in mid-air. There simply is nothing for them to attach themselves to, but kingdom context revealed to us through kingdom reasoning provides a setting and a sense to all human experience. The believer is delivered from the sheer randomness of self-willed insight and supposition and is placed into the very center of God's revealed will.

Kingdom reasoning is "Christo-centric." That means we see the promise and context of Jesus Christ in all the scriptures, both Old and New Testament, as the primary interpretation and application of all biblical truth.

> *"Christ is the key to all truths. Without Him the Bible would be a dead book. Without Him we would never understand the Scriptures. When we are confronted with difficult passages in God's word, we will receive marvelous light if we can relate them to Christ."*
>
> WATCHMAN NEE, *The Mystery of Creation*

Being Christo-centric also means we see all events in this age as having the promise of clarity only through Christ's continuing presence amongst us.

The wilderness thinking found in the first generation of the rescued children of Israel robbed them of their sense of God's abiding presence among them. The result was that the daily pangs of their stomach or their fear of their future status caused them to despise their miraculous deliverance. They wanted a God with a different purpose—a God of their choosing (Psalm 106:43).

We must reverse the in-roads of wilderness thinking amongst us. We must expose the roots of these co-mingled doctrines. Kingdom understanding must never be compromised or merged with a man-made agenda.

"We would see Jesus" (John 12:21) is the true heart of all believers. And *"We would see Jesus"* is the first prayer of kingdom reasoning. It is a prayer our Father longs to answer in each of us!

TOWARDS THE RELIGION OF TOMORROW

"I know your works: you are neither cold nor hot. Would that you were cold or hot! So, because you are lukewarm, and neither cold nor hot, I will spew you out of my mouth."

REVELATION 3:15-16

"The only significance in life consists in helping establish the Kingdom of God."

LEO TOLSTOY

WE ARE THE vessels that contain the water of life for the whole world. Water left to itself becomes room or ambient temperature. It becomes lukewarm. It takes energy, a constant stream of energy, to either heat up a liquid or remove heat (refrigerate) a liquid. Spiritually, this energy source is the Holy Spirit (John 16:14) and the children of God are the servants who fill vessels, empty vessels, remove obstacles, etc., so that the Holy Spirit is free to operate and develop the kingdom characteristics needed in any particular circumstance (2 Corinthians 4:7, John 2:7, John 11:39-44, Philippians 2:17, Proverbs 11:25, John 13:14).

Both hot and cold water have their uses. You wouldn't offer a weary traveler who has just come in from the desert a cup of hot water to refresh him (Matthew 10:42); nor would you attempt to remove the dirt from your hands with cold water. Both kinds of water have their uses. Both have their seasons.

In the arid climate of Palestine, during the ministry of our Lord, there were only two ways to ensure that water was cold: it would have to be either freshly drawn from a well or collected from a flowing stream. It would represent a special act of kindness and ministry in order to present someone with fresh, clear, cold water.

Today in the church we are often blind to the significance of offering the hurting of this world fresh, cool water. We think that by merely reciting biblical passages over someone or some situation we have presented God's blessing or stated God's "cause." Often we give little more than lukewarm words to the world-weary and we secretly hope that this will suffice. It seldom, if ever, does.

To call oneself a Christian is to call oneself by no other name, both in this age and in the age to come. This doesn't mean that we melodramatically disown or dishonor our earthly heritage. It means we trade in what we once thought about ourselves, what we once drew strength and identity from, and place it at the foot of the cross. We offer it to Jesus, not because it was evil, but because it was incomplete (Psalm 119:96, Philippians 3:7) and we recognize it as such. To call oneself a Christian is to call oneself a servant of all humankind.

Sadly, too many people in the "proper" church have forgotten the incarnational imperative of Christ that continues throughout this age (2 Corinthians 4:10, John 14:20-24). Even now, the sons of men need to say, "We would see Jesus." Jesus would have that personal presence revealed through you and me. We are to be an authentic representation of the true King of this earth.

The church, the Christian "religion," is not simply acoustic perfume designed to blot out the dissonance and white noise of personal sin and cultural chaos. We are the difference makers (Acts 17:6). We are the salt (Matthew 5:13). We are responsible for the destiny of all men because we are entrusted with the message and spiritual gifts that can lead men to eternal life.

Many believers think that by simply denouncing the word "religion" they have then achieved some great spiritual breakthrough. But the word itself means devoted service to God. So what is it that we are trying to say to the world by denouncing such a word? Is it that the "Self" remains the standard of all theology and that some notion of a personalized Jesus replaces the kingdom calling of the Father? Heaven forbid such simpleness!

The Great Commission (Matthew 28:18-20) commands us as a body to preach and make disciples of all nations. This is the beginning of our kingdom mission. This calling is a command that must reside in the heart and mind of each believer. Our calling should never solely be replaced with a prepackaged or an orchestrated scheme. Christ never reduced His presence to a formula or gimmickry and, likewise, His presence in us must not be so reduced. Think of "making disciples" in the same sense as "making vessels." What are vessels meant to hold? What is their function in the household now? What does God desire for us to contain of Himself in the midst of this generation? This is the other side of the kingdom. This is kingdom content and kingdom character and that is what the religion of tomorrow must have as

opposed to the lukewarm slogans of limited vision one encounters so often in present day religion.

The religion of tomorrow must contain the same creative daring found only in the presence of Christ. The church of tomorrow must renounce any acceptance of the horrors of the human existence as something necessary and legitimate. We must recognize our response as the response of Christ Himself and stop anticipating our collective escape velocity by the perceived wickedness around us. The church doesn't escape the gates of hell through some atmospheric trap door. We represent the victory of Christ, not a well-thought-out strategic retreat.

Jesus Christ is the same yesterday, today, and tomorrow. We, His church, are called to maturity, sacrifice, and authentic service. Such a calling is not measurable in mediocrity or sameness. Our mission is dynamic and fresh (Romans 12:11).

The religion of tomorrow will preach the Gospel of the Eternal Christ and His kingdom:

- WITH WISDOM. This includes the wisdom of the prophets, Proverbs, Psalms, the clear teachings of Jesus, and the application of Paul, the Apostles, and the Church Fathers. Wisdom and love are the supreme expression of kingdom power and kingdom presence (1 Corinthians 13:4-7, Proverbs 3:13-23).

- WITH PRAYER. This prayer must be daring, intimate, informed, continuous, passionate, and undistracted, both privately and in fellowship. Conversations approaching the heart of God must be fueled with wonder, perfumed with worship, and purged of self-conceit.

- WITH AUTHORITY. Truth will be the hallmark of a church that avoids the vain speculation and corrupt doctrines of men. Only the truth of God's word can authenticate the authority of our call and service. The authentic community of faith under the direction of the Holy Spirit is equipped to be the custodian and advocate of God's word.

- WITH COURAGE. Charlatans, hustlers, and braggarts must be cut off from the community of faith. Spiritual falsehood and vanity should be rooted out fearlessly wherever they may be found. The true Gospel must be spread, person to person, throughout all nations and tribes.

- WITH UNITY. God continues to hold the door open between all His children and within His church. This is not a call for empty ecumenical sentiment, but a command from God Himself to show effective unity as one of the evidences of His Son's lordship (John 17:11). The Holy Spirit stands ready to lead the church forward in authentic unity. True unity begins with a clear understanding of the here-and-now purposes of God and His kingdom.

- WITH DIGNITY. We are to go forward in the dignity of holiness, in the dignity of the presence of Christ, in the dignity of simple, contented lives committed to kingdom excellence. We are to uphold the dignity of the scriptures and the ancient landmarks of our faith, the dignity of words fitly spoken. We will revere the dignity of life; the dignity of the

sick, the aged, the unborn, the orphan, the refugee,
the broken hearted, the poor, the prisoner, and the
prodigal. We will honor the dignity of our human
design and the creative power of our Sovereign
God.

- AND WITH LOVE. For God so loved the world/For
  we so loved the Son/For we so loved one another.

Tomorrow must not be like today. Tomorrow
must be more like Jesus (John 3:30).

Tomorrow must seek the grace and power to
reveal the purposes of God and the presence of
Christ to all men.

The kingdom presence of God is to be known
passionately in the soul of every believer. The
kingdom presence of God is in evidence when two
or more are gathered in His name. His presence is
quiet yet it is eloquent; it is simple and practical yet
astonishing and powerful; it is hidden in the lives
of those most despised and yet it grows majestically
in the midst of all living creation. To abide in His
presence and participate in His being is to experience
the Eternal Life of the Eternal Father (John 14-17).

And so, we humble ourselves…we empty ourselves…and we pray, "Thy kingdom come, Thy will
be done…come Lord Jesus." As even now, through
grace and by faith, we enter the kingdom presence of
God.

TO THE FOOT OF
GOD'S THRONE

FROM THE FOOT
OF THE CROSS

IN THE INSTANT
I FIRST BELIEVED.

NOTES